I Didn't That™ Know

Why We Say the Things We Say

from
"All Gussied Up"
to
"Under the Weather"

Volume 1

Word and Phrase Origins
Compiled and Edited by

Karlen Evins

K Rose
publishing

K. Rose Publishing
P.O. Box 24
Alexandria, Tennessee 37012
Copyright © 2009 by K. Rose Publishing, Inc.
www.karlenevins.com

Designed by Karlen Evins & Dave Turner
www.digitaldave.com

Manufactured in the United States of America

Library of Congress Control Number: 2009905351
ISBN-13 9780963547446
UPC 617258002337

Parts of this book were previously published by Simon & Schuster.
Series and revised editions property of K. Rose Publishing, Inc

For Teddy

A Word of Thanks

An ancient African proverb once said, "It takes a village to raise a child." By the same token, it takes a village to create a book.

Ask any author and you will find that our books are our children... the birthing of each bringing a village together (in our case, the village idiots maybe... but hey, a village was involved)!

Theses pages cannot hold the debt of gratitude I owe the team that helped bring this child to life.

To Teddy Bart, my co-host, business partner and best friend, thank you for believing in me when I was just a pup... still *wet behind the ears*. This one's for you!

To Digital Dave Turner, for your tireless, creative spirit, your Tigger-like enthusiasm and the endless laughter... thank you! You have made this journey a joy.

To my lifelong friend Ria Baker, whose creativity never ceases to amaze me... thank you for the life you have given these pages, and the love you have given my life.

To the editing team of Miss Helen, Dave, Elliott and Lance, thanks for those edits! Your sharp eyes and keen sense of punctuation helped make a manuscript from radio scripts. ('Twas not an easy task, I know.)

To Ike, Minsky and Bella, thank you for reminding us that walks in the park are a cure-all for everything.

And to my angels, helpers and guides... thank you for dancing on our walls at sunset, reminding us that you are always and forever in our midst.

A Note from the Author

This little book was born many moons ago as a part of a local radio show that originated in Nashville, Tennessee. When asked to produce something light to toss into our otherwise often heated political debate, I offered up a personal hobby of mine: collecting stories behind the things we say.

The show's host loved it, and soon our audience did too. I had long been collecting words and phrases, many coming from my own Southern upbringing, many picked up as a by-product of my passion for finding used book stores whenever I traveled.

As often happens when you least expect it, the feature took on a life of its own, with the most common response to each story being, *"I Didn't Know That!"* So the show's host dubbed the feature just that. And the rest, as they say, is history.

The first edition of this book was a small, self-published work composed on a Lisa 2 E (Mac) computer in between auditions, weather casts and the part time radio gigs I juggled in the early 90s. A few thousand books later, I stashed the project in my attic, as the demands of a full time broadcasting career left no time for my little self-publishing hobby.

Fifteen years later the book made its way to the Big Apple as part of a much larger world than I could have imagined. From this came newspaper columns, internet blogs, and ultimately a return to radio -- this time at network levels. But through it all, it was the feedback from everyday people that kept calling me home.

For this reason, *I Didn't Know That* returns to its roots as a simple little book, cranked out from our own little shop, with new stories, fun features, and additional twists that continue to evolve as others share their own accounts of words, sayings and expressions they too, have picked up along the way.

Some expressions vary culture to culture; others gain new meaning with time. And for some, there is no way to know for certain who said what first. But the stories continue still. And if there is any way to keep these stories alive, I'm all for it.

And that is what drives this little compendium of a book about why we say the things we say, fondly referred to still as *I Didn't Know That!*

For those likewise fascinated with the stories, the legends, the folklore, the myth...I welcome your letters, your comments and your emails. As with any good friendship, shared stories bring us closer together--and so it goes in our never ending dance with a language so colorful, it sparks life with each new discovery.

May these words, phrases and expressions bring joy to your travels and laughter to your conversations. And maybe, just maybe, before you reach the final page, you too, will find yourself saying...

"I Didn't Know That!"

Happy Reading~

Karlen

Introduction

Throughout this journey, when asked "What prompted your interest in these sayings?" I refer to a story told to me by my Papaw. It involves a young couple and a holiday meal and a tradition tied thereto centering around a young bride's custom of trimming the ends off her holiday ham.

When the new husband asked his wife why, her response was, "Because my mom always did." When he asked his mother-in-law the same, he got the same answer: "Because *my* mom always did." And when seated across the table from his aging, sweet grandmother-in-law he asked a third time, "Why do you trim the ends off your ham?"She held her hands before her as if to explain, "Well, in my day the pans were only this big."

It's a simple little story that makes a great big point and that is that so much of what we do and even more of what we say is pure habit. We've done it or said it for so long we've forgotten where it came from (provided we ever knew to start with).

But remembering is a worthwhile journey. Not only is it fun, but it makes life more meaningful when we share our stories.

Such is my thinking behind *I Didn't Know That*.

May this book bring you as much joy in the reading as it has brought me in the writing.

Here's to keeping the stories alive.

All Gussied Up

To be *all gussied up* means you're decked out in your Sunday finest. So in case you've ever wondered, "Just what IS a gussy anyway?" Well I'm here to tell you. (No, the word has nothing to do with hussies; but it does trace back to a gusset.)

A gusset (from the French word *gousset*, which means they probably didn't pronounce the "t" in the original) is a triangular piece of material, inserted into a garment to enhance its fit and form. Any woman who gusseted her dress, did so to improve her appearance, thus to be *all gussied up* meant she was dressed to the nines... (But wait! That's another story... And you can find it on page 30!)

All Your Eggs in One Basket

To put *all your eggs in one basket* is to risk everything *in one fell swoop,* so to speak... (Here we go again. See page 91.)

We credit this one to businessman and philanthropist Andrew Carnegie, once the richest man in the world.

Carnegie is said to have credited the phrase to Mark Twain, in a simple reference to not banking everything you've got on one single outcome.

The expression was in fact, cited in Mark Twain's Pudd'nhead Wilson Calendar (1854). And just so you know, the original reads:

"Put all your eggs in one basket, and watch that basket!"

(Gotta love that Mark Twain!)

Amateur

Of all the expressions in this book, it's the word *amateur* that I like the best.

Just so you know, the word derives from the Latin word *amator*, which translated, means "a lover."

Today the word connotes one lacking enough experience to qualify as a professional, but the original meaning dealt more with motive than ranking.

The first *amateur* engaged in a pastime for the *love* of that pastime, as opposed to taking on the task purely for the sake of money. For the artist or the athlete today that truly loves the profession he or she has chosen, it's a toss up:

--professional (in it for the money) or
--amateur (lover of the process)?
(My question: must it be an either/or?)

3

(to run) Amuck

To run amuck means you're out of control. The image is that of one running about in a wild, frantic frenzy. And the origin of the word traces halfway around the world.

Dating back to the 16th century when European explorers encountered the Malay people, story has it the natives became very excited at their arrival and yelled the words:

"Amoq! Amoq!"

(Another story suggests the natives were prone to depression, and their herbal remedies made for hallucinogenic outbursts of such frenzies, but this is not confirmed.)

Regardless, the words interpret "Kill! Kill!" And from that same impassioned phrase, *amuck* is today, our watered down version of what was once a murderous fighting call of native tribesmen running wild and scared.

Apple Pie Order

Some say it has to do with the apples *in* the pies; others say it's the arrangement of apple pies *on* the shelf. (And there are even some who credit a French phrase: *nappes pliees*, which dates back to the 1600s and has something to do with neatly folded linens.)

But the bottom line is: *apple pie order* means you've got your ducks in a row, (which is another expression entirely).

Regardless, we Americans like to trace our version to pioneer days, when wives of the frontiersmen did their baking at the first of the week.

Arranging the apples within the pie, and arranging the pies on the shelves once baked, were both neat and orderly procedures, thus providing our neat and tidy *apple pie order* meaning we still hold today.

As the Crow Flies

An expression that means the shortest distance between two points, *as the crow flies* is country-speak for "Head straight that-a-way."

Trace it back far enough and you'll find this all too familiar Southern expression is actually nautical in origin.

What most people don't know is that British ships of old carried cages of crows because crows (get this) loathe large bodies of water and will fly straight to land once freed to do so! (No doubt this came in pretty handy when you needed to spot the direction in which to set your sails in a time that was pre-satellite.)

And for what it's worth, this is the very same reason we call the lookout of a ship the *crow's nest!* (Little extra tidbit of trivia there. Two for the price of one!)

Backseat Driver

Truth be told, most *backseat drivers* aren't in the back seat. They're technically riding shotgun (i.e., in the passenger seat, so very annoyingly next to you).

The term suggests a complainer or someone who thinks he can see better from where he sits than from where the driver is perched (and doesn't hesitate to tell you so).

But the original *backseat drivers* weren't complainers at all. Matter of fact, they *were* in the back, and they *could* see better because this was their job.

In days of the early fire engine, *backseat drivers* were those in charge of watching the ladder as engines rushed to the scene. As quick turns and abrupt stops were cause for accidents, a *backseat driver* was as vital a part of the fire team as the fire fighters themselves!

Baker's Dozen

An expression that means thirteen, (not twelve), a *baker's dozen* traces back as far as ancient Egypt, though it was the British Parliament that actually passed the law that popularized the notion and gave meaning to the phrase as we use it today.

As heavy penalties were fined those bakers who shortchanged their customers by selling them lighter loaves of bread, in 1266, England passed strict weight restriction laws to ensure bakers never came up short.

Since weights could vary per loaf, it became customary for bakers to add a 13th loaf for good measure, and it is from this protective move that a *baker's dozen* became a more colorful way of saying, "Thirteen, please!"

Balderdash

A word meaning a senseless muddle of words, the earliest recorded reference to "*Balderdash!*" came from a frothy campaign ad, dating back to the late 16th century.

It was Barber's Balderdash that first coined the term describing their "light and frothy" shaving liquid. Perhaps derived from the Danish word *balder* (meaning noisy or a loud clatter), what we do know is that it was John Taylor, the "water poet" who gave "umph" to the word when describing a beer mixed with wine, calling the concoction: *Balderdash!*

Since then, be it liquids or be it language, the word has come to represent an impossible combination of energies.

(And didn't that word lend itself nicely to the board game bearing the same name?)

Ballpark Number

A guestimation at best, *ballpark numbers* have a couple of stories of origin.

One hails from the game of baseball itself, where being *in the ballpark* meant you were within the bounds of play (the business analogy being you're in the negotiating zone).

Another origin traces the expression to the 1800s when ballparks were home to large events, both sports-related and otherwise.

Political candidates used ballparks for rallies, as these provided ample space for a crowd.

But as no tickets were sold for such events, reporters could only guestimate in *ballpark numbers* the attendance. Invariably, one party would overestimate for the sake of the press, prompting the rival party to, in turn, do the same. As a result, *ballpark figures* became synonymous with any rough, unprovable count.

The Bane of My Existence

The bane of my existence connotes one of constant irritation, and the expression is most often used to describe a person who is a perpetual source of misery. Like so many expressions today, its meaning has been diluted over time-- the original *bane* being a far deadlier proposition.

From the Middle English *bana*, the base word means "a slayer" (or what today we might call an assassin or a murderer).

By the 14th century, *bane* described various forms of poisonous plants, such as *wolfbane* or *henbane*. The resulting effect was no different from *rats bane* (aka rat poison)-- an ingredient known to kill a person even today (or at the very least, make his life miserable).

Bated Breath

Easy to look under baited, isn't it? (As in baited hook, baited trap...) But baited breath?

Fortunate for us all, *bated* in this context is a simple hyphenation for *abated*, a word that means to lower or depress.

It's a word we don't use much today. Rather, you are best to reference your literary classics to grasp its prosaic essence. Just add the word to breath, and you're talking about breathing that is "subdued owing to something emotional." In other words, something dreadful lies ahead.

Made popular by Shakespeare, who first used the phrase in his "Merchant of Venice," the line he penned went like this:

"With bated breath,
and whispering humblenesse…"

The good news is abated breath (as opposed to breath that was baited) makes far more sense than the mental image most assume at first blush.

Beating around the Bush

Not to be confused with beating the bushes, *beating around the bush* is a different idiom entirely. But as you might imagine, both expressions trace their lineage to the sport of hunting.

As most hunters will attest, it is sometimes necessary to scare game (particularly birds) into running or flying before you can shoot, thus beating the bushes we borrowed from a customary hunting procedure of old.

But *beating around the bush* derives from the hunter who really did not enjoy killing for sport, who discovered that in *beating around the bush* he could scare off the game so as to avoid any confrontation.

It's that same noise-making distraction that gives this phrase our meaning today.

Beyond the Pale

Not the kind of pale that suggests you're sickly. The pale in the expression *beyond the pale* has nothing whatsoever to do with pasty, ghostly or white.

Instead, the pale in *beyond the pale* we take from the Latin word *palus*, which was a stake or boundary marker surrounding the territory under rule by a certain nation. (Think palings in your white picket fences and you start to get the picture.)

Such palings or boundary markers were especially common in Roman times. Thus, the social outcast believed to be living beyond the bounds of societal or moral decency was literally exiled *beyond the pale*, or beyond the confines of civilization as determined by the townspeople.

Blimp

Nope, Goodyear didn't invent this one (despite what they tell you on Monday Night Football). And for you language buffs, some say the word *blimp* is onomatopoeic -- big word meaning the word imitates the sound it describes. (Think: Meow. Crash! Bang!)

By the same token, they say if you're close enough to thump this thing, the sound would go "blimp!"

But the more important fact to know is that the non-rigid aircraft we today call a blimp originated in 1914, and was the one of two non-rigid airships being tested in England (namely, the *A-limp* and the *B-limp*).

The former never quite made it off the ground, but version *"B"* of the limp aircraft became famous and is today fondly referred to as *blimp!*

Bringing Home the Bacon

The British credit this one to an Old English custom wherein married couples making it one full year with no fighting, were gifted a side of bacon for the feat. (Such an anniversary present, no?)

Now whether that custom gave us our current meaning for *bringing home the bacon*, I can't say.

The more popular explanation is that *bringing home the bacon*, is purely American in origin, dating back to the greased pig contests of old county fairs.

As the catcher was the keeper, the expression speaks for itself.

Cahoots

To be in *cahoots* with somebody means you're in some sort of unofficial, shady partnership (i.e., a deal not totally on the up-and-up, if you know what I mean).

Trace the word to its original roots and you find that *cahoots* (or "kajuetes" as they were called in medieval times), literally translated to mean "little cabins."

As these little cabins were reportedly occupied by bandits and robbers, "kajuetes" (or *cahoots)*, over time became synonymous with these cabin-lookin' attack-planning centers.

But in reality, it was the goings-on *inside* the cabins that became synonymous with the cabins themselves. Today the word *cahoots* still refers to any shady partnership or less than honorable scheme.

Catch as Catch Can

A phrase meaning you make the most of things as best you can, *catch as catch can* in its earliest sense was a form of wrestling that originated in Lancashire, England.

Some will tell you it was the precursor to our modern day pro-wrestling, but regardless, *catch wrestling* was a blend of martial arts and combat training that took the country by storm when carnivals, traveling shows and public exhibitions made it popular in the years between The Civil War and The Great Depression.

With a focus on clinching and swift ground moves, *catch wrestling* was said to incorporate everything from jujitsu to judo.

The goal of the sport was to make the most of any situation in the moment that it happened, which is precisely what is meant when we use the phrase today.

Charley Horse

It's a cramp like none other, and it hurts like heck. It makes you limp, 'cause it happens in your leg. Our Aussie cousins call it corked leg (or "corker" for short), which is cute... but not as cute as our name, for our name has a story!

Believe it or not, Charley was an actual horse! And when he got old, his owner decided to loan him to the keeper of the White Sox ball park in Chicago in 1890 to pull the roller that laid the chalk lines for the baseball games there.

Because old Charley was not in the prime of his life, he limped; and before long the crowd began to refer to any limping player on the team as *Old Charley Horse.*

19

Chess Pie

Chess pie, in case you're not from the South, is that lovely (if not deadly) concoction of butter, sugar and eggs that will put you into a diabetic coma if you aren't careful. Its basic ingredients rival our traditional pecan pie (chess being a similar, though less expensive, non-topped version).

Several stories exist, including one that says the original name was not chess at all, but "chest" pie (said to be made with so much sugar you could store them in a pie chest without refrigeration).

But the more soulful version credits our country's best source on cooking wisdom: plantation slaves. Folklore, maybe, but story has it that it was a humble kitchen servant whose delicacy warmed the whole house. When asked, "What kind of pie is that?" The answer was: *"It's jes' pie."*

And from this, a legend was born.

Chewing the Fat

Like so many of our colorful expressions, *chewing the fat* is another that originated on the high seas.

(Think pre-refrigeration. Think early days of sailing. Think foods carried on long trips that required no ice cubes. O.K. Stop thinking now, or you might get seasick.)

So...Are you with me so far? If so, you already know that one such non-refrigerated favorite was salt pork. And as a luxury, no part of this meat was going to waste (including the skin). Thus fat became common fare between meals and even meal substitutes.

Late 1870s -- chewing the fat became *the* catch phrase for idle chatter that originally accompanied the *real* fat chewing that took place aboard ships of old.

Clean as a Whistle

You might not think of a whistle as a standard for measuring cleanliness, but if you ever tried to make one you'd understand the phrase completely.

Keep in mind the first whistles were not those you see around the necks of football coaches and referees. Nope. The very first whistles were made of reeds, tall and slender.

To obtain the pure wind sound derived from a reed whistle, the tube of the thing had to be totally free of debris -- meaning it was clean, clear and dry.

By the same token to have a thing *clean as a whistle* today means it's as orderly as possible, with absolutely nothing obstructing its passageway.

Cocktail

In case you're ever asked at a cocktail party, the inventor of the cocktail was one Antoine Amedee Peychaud -- a druggist from the West Indies who came to New Orleans in the late 1700s.

Famous for an invention concocted of Peychaud's Bitters, Antoine once mixed a special drink of bitters and brandy in an egg cup known as a *coquetier* (pronounced "kok-tyay").

So popular became the drink that soon, cafes and bars in New Orleans picked up on the concoction, and with this, the first *cocktails* were born!

Coconut

The largest nut on earth (not to be confused with your favorite politician), the *coco* in *coconut* has nothing to do with coco beans, Coco Beach or even Coco-Puffs!

Nope. The *coco* in *coconut* was so named thanks to a Portuguese word that means "grinning face."

Dating back to the 15th century, the original reference of *coconut* was made to that of a human head. History traces the name to a Portuguese explorer who, upon sailing around the islands of the Indian Ocean, noted that this nut was not only the approximate size of the human head, but (given the height of the palm trees on which they grew) was said to resemble smiling faces from a distance.

Cold Shoulder

The first *cold shoulder* referred to a cold shoulder of meat, given to a sojourner who might stop along the course of his travels to ask for food.

As mutton was the common course of old English farmhouses, it was customary when trying to be kind (though not *too* kind) to hand any stranger who came knocking, a cold shoulder of meat before sending him on his way.

Anything more (like a warm meal) would have indicated an invitation to stick around a bit longer. On the other hand, a *cold shoulder* was a sign that the traveler would be fed, but should expect no more.

Crocodile Tears

Crocodile tears are those insincere tears we've come to equate with false emotions. But biologically speaking, crocodile tears are quite literal (at least for the croc).

Curiously, a crocodile does indeed cry as it devours its prey. But before you get all sentimental, you should know that the croc's crying has nothing to do with his emotional sensitivities.

Nope. What you need to know is that as a crocodile eats, his food is pressed to the top of his mouth, causing pressure against glands known as the lachrymals.

These glands secrete a tear-like substance that flow from the crocodile's eyes, and from this reptilian biological activity, do we today draw our meaning for *crocodile tears*.

Dandelions

No, this cute little flower didn't get its name from looking like an actual lion! Matter of fact, the *dande* part has nothing to do with our word dandy at all.

Instead, it all goes back to the French where this fuzzy little flower was called *dent de lion*, NOT for the flower, but for the leaves, thought to look like jagged lion's teeth.

Dent (base word for all things dental in our language today) *de* (of the) *lion*, literally translates: "tooth of the lion."

For what it's worth, the French word for dandelion today is *pissenlit*, which when translated literally means "urinate in bed" (supposedly named for the dandelion's diuretic qualities).

Deadbeat

To be clear, the word *deadbeat* is probably one of our easiest to explain, as the word derives from what the expression was designed to convey, namely those out to beat their debts.

Deadbeaters were people who avoided their creditors by leaving their debts behind. In the early days of this country, there were two ways to shirk your financial obligations: (1) declaring bankruptcy. (2) move out of the colony where the debt was incurred.

Those opting for the latter, were called "debt beaters," which in time, shortened and mispronounced, became -- *deadbeats!*

Dog Days

These are the hottest days of summer.

Those dog-gone *dog days* will have you sweatin' like a dog (but this has nothing to do with why we call 'em *dog days*--stay with us).

Let us be clear. On our half of the planet, in our half of the hemisphere, the hottest days of summer fall under the constellation Canis Major, in which Sirius (also known as the Dog Star) is the brightest star. This star falls just below Orion's belt, in case you've got your telescope handy.

Now to be astrologically correct (if not just really snooty) you might call 'em, *"Cuniculares Dies,"* instead of just *dog days*... (*canicula* being the Roman word for dog and all). The Romans believed this star was responsible for the scorching heat of summer.

But if you want anyone to know what in the heck you're talking about, you'd probably just call 'um *dog days* like the rest of us do.

Dressed to the Nines

No, this doesn't mean that on a scale from one to ten, a person dressed to the nines is one point shy of perfection.

The expression is British in origin, and when spoken correctly (with a very proper accent) was "Dressed to thy'n eyes." (Quite obviously in reference to one spiffed up from head to toe!)

Leave it to us to mispronounce it a bit, and make a popular expression out of wording that otherwise, makes absolutely no sense!

Drinks Like a Fish

A phrase dating back to the mid 1600s, this one describes a person who imbibes in too much alcohol, which begs the question: *"Do fish really drink?"*

Technically, no. But fish do derive their sustenance from the waters in which they swim, which is to say, their happy hour is always at hand (or fin, as the case may be).

Some credit Fletcher and Shirley's "Night Walker" for the line:

"Give me the bottle. I can drink like a fish now... like an elephant later."

Sadly (but not surprisingly) the elephant analogy didn't quite catch on. But the fish part did, which is why drunken fish hold a cherished place in our language today.

Drunker than Cooter Brown

For starters, those of us who knew him best called him *Cootie*!

(But this is beside the point.)

The name synonymous with all things drunken, hails from *Cooter Brown's Tavern & Oyster Bar* in New Orleans (or so they tell me).

So here's what I found...

Cooter Brown lived in Civil War times, somewhere near the Mason-Dixon line.

With family on both sides, and hoping never-ever to be drafted (by the North or the South), Cooter opted for drunkenness to avoid the inevitable.

Ever since, drunken standards everywhere have been measured against Cooter Brown's extended binges, the likes of which netted us the colorful expression:

Drunker that Cooter (aka Cootie) Brown!

Dyed in the Wool

Anyone working with wool knows that when you attempt to dye an item after it is already spun and woven into cloth, the odds of having an even, color-fast result are slim to none.

The proper way to dye wool is to color the raw material before it is ever woven. By the same token, one said to be *dyed in the wool* is a person who is thoroughly indoctrinated with a belief, believing in his cause through and through, leaving no gaps, no holes, no openings for any change in his opinion.

Earmark

It was long, long ago in a far-away land (otherwise known as England) that farmers found a way to identify stolen livestock in an effort to prevent thieves from stealing their sheep, cattle and pigs.

The solution? Mark the ears of their own animals with the farmer's own initials or the farm's branded logo.

What do you know? It worked!

Almost too well, sadly...

In time *ear-marking* became such the solution that for a period of time, anyone caught in the act of stealing an earmarked animal, was earmarked himself!

(Now 'ears to a punishment that fits the crime... Literally!)

34

Ear to the Ground

They say we can thank our early American Indians for this one...

Perhaps you were told (as some legends have it) that keeping *an ear to the ground* was the way Native American Indians listened for the sound of approaching horses.

But Native American Indians will tell you the custom had less to do with battle strategies ... more to do with their sacred spiritual beliefs.

The belief was the Great Spirit resided in nature; thus, land was sacred. By the same token, listening to Mother Earth was in essence, a prayer.

In other words, an *ear to the ground* was a centering gesture that kept you silently listening for the sweetest heartbeat of all -- namely Mother Earth.

Face the Music

So let's think....

Who faces music for a living? Symphony conductors? Band leaders?

Yes. But as you have probably surmised by now, a person facing the music is not having a good day. Nope. Obviously from the connotation of the phrase, music-facing isn't pleasant. Nor was it when the expression originated.

Background of the phrase traces to the U.S. Army. The music referenced: *Rogue's March*, which was the tune played when an offender was cast out of the service.

As disgraceful a moment as one could experience, to *face the music* means you accept your disgrace and turn in your stripes.

Fair to Middlin'

An expression found in American literature from Mark Twain to Louisa May Alcott, the phrase *fair to middlin'* dates back to the mid 1800s, though the original, it appears, dates back at least three decades earlier.

The term, which was popularized as an American expression, designates a quality of grade in certain markets including, but not limited to: cotton, flour, meal and other such commodities.

More specifically, the phrase seems to have originated with cotton grades, the sequence running from best (fine) to good (fair) to middlin' (meaning slightly less than fair).

Thus, *fair to middlin'* (meaning an intermediate quality grade), was from this reference in the cotton industry, adapted to the more common nomenclature of the English language.

Fiasco

By definition, a *fiasco* describes some utterly foolish failure, and to be fair, the first fiascos *were* in fact, failures. But not in the way we use the word today.

Instead, the original *fiascos* were glass blunders -- simple goofs that often wound up having greater uses than the originally designed work of art itself.

Tracing back to glass blowers of Renaissance Italy, tradition held that if a bottle had a flaw, it was set aside to be reworked into a flask (or "fiasco" in Italian).

Not as artsy, but far more practical in function, the salvaged, re-created works became useful in a whole new way.

Fighting Fire with Fire

American in origin, and one of the few we carried down exactly as we coined it, *fighting fire with fire* means you use the same tactic as your attacker to fight back. But the original expression was about as literal as it gets.

When early American settlers, in dealing with prairie fires, learned that by setting ablaze a strip of land in the fire's path, they could often lessen its impact, *fighting fire with fire* became synonymous with fighting defensively with the offense's method.

As blazes hitting barren land had nothing to feed upon, they were more readily controlled. Soon the phrase became defined as "a dangerous measure to solve a dangerous problem."

Flash in the Pan

Think muzzle-loaded flintlock muskets of Revolutionary days; then think small, little pan of a space under the trigger, that held priming powder used to ignite the spark.

Now imagine if you will, just how many times this little spark didn't do the trick, as too many times, when you pulled the trigger on those early muskets, nothing happened.

"Why," you ask? Because the hammer striking the flint did not generate a spark strong enough to ignite the powder.

Watch the spark fizzle in this shallow pan holding the powder, and you know precisely where our image of *flash in the pan* came from. To this day we hold its meaning to be something that dazzles, but doesn't get the job done!

Fly-by-Night

Mention a *fly-by-night* and you automatically know you're talking about someone or something slightly shady if not downright dishonorable.

Fly-by-nights reference those businesses or business people that are here today, gone tomorrow. But believe it or not, the first *fly-by-nights* were witches!

As witches travel by broom (and at night, no less), the reference was to something or someone up to no good.

But if you're ever in England, be careful when tossing this expression about.

For in Britain, a *fly-by-night* is slang for prostitute -- one who does her business in the dark of night, while making herself scarce by the light of day.

Freeloader

The first *freeloading* (as in free food, free drink, free anything-you-could-sponge-off your pals) took place in the pubs of merry old England. The unspoken rule of the day had each regular paying one round apiece, until everyone had contributed to the overall tab.

The person who drank his rounds then left the pub before his turn to pay got loaded for free, hence the term: *freeloader*.

Curiously, there's another version of this, more apt to be used in Northern England, wherein the same type person was called a pint-shyer (for being the one who was shy his payment due for the pint he consumed).

Garden

Garden is a word so common you probably don't think it has a story, but it does.

(And a meaningful one at that!)

Deriving its name from the Old French word, *jardin*, the first gardens were created by medieval monks. These plots were set aside for food and flowers, in tribute to the garden of all gardens: The Garden of Eden.

Providing both food and serenity for the active, yet meditative disciplines of monastic life, gardens soon became a staple of every abbey and monastery throughout Europe.

As walls and fences were erected to protect these sacred plots, these "guarded" lands soon became known as *gardens*... a word that still today represents a piece of earth set aside for life and all things growth.

Getting Your Goat

Get someone's goat, and you're getting on someone's nerves! (It means you are annoying.)

But the first "goat-getters" were far more deliberate in their ploy.

It was discovered in the early days of horse racing that goats had a calming effect on the more high strung pacers entering the paddocks. As a result, savvy owners began placing goats in their horse's stall, in order to calm the horse before each race.

While the two critters made for great roommates, it didn't take long for conniving opponents to learn that by *getting someone's goat*, you could alter the race entirely.

Today the phrase is just as unnerving for humans as it was back then for race horses. (And no one's even stopped to consider what it's done to the poor goat!)

Goblin

Now several stories exist for *goblins*--those mischievous, gnome-like creatures always up to no good.

But of all the stories, one of the more colorful, if not our most popular, traces the word, *goblin*, back to the early 1400s, to a day when a beautiful bright red fabric was introduced in Paris, France by Gilles and Jehan Gobelin.

Story has it, that this cloth was so stunning that Louis XIV declared the Gobelin factory a royal business, at which point the superstitious and jealous locals around town started rumors suggesting the brothers sold their souls to the devil in exchange for their sudden good fortune.

As a result, the Gobelins were ostracized. Over time, their name became synonymous with any evil or mischievous being.

God Bless You

If you've ever wondered why people say *"God Bless You!"* right after you sneeze, well... good question! Here's your answer.

Ancient spiritual belief once held that a person's soul could exit the body under certain stressful conditions (i.e., physical or emotional duress). Of course, the ultimate parting of body and spirit would be death. But on those more temporary occasions, a person could still find his soul outside his body given the right set of conditions.

One such situation involved the common sneeze, wherein it was believed that if the sneeze were strong enough, a person could literally blast his spirit right out of his body!

To ensure that no bad spirits moved into the vacancy while the house was left vacant, *God Bless You* was said to keep the temple clean, so soul and body could rightfully reunite.

46

Golf

Some say GOLF is an acronym standing for *Gentlemen Only; Ladies Forbidden.* (Personally, I like the story. Odds are good it's not true.)

As for the game itself, some credit shepherds hitting rocks with crooks. Others credit the Romans. (Oh, and the Dutch had a game played by hitting a rock across frozen canals.) But *golf,* as we play the game today, does indeed trace its roots to the famed St. Andrews of Scotland.

We do know that golf was so popular in the Middle Ages that King James II banned it in 1457 when an obsession for the game wreaked havoc on archery training.

As for the name itself, etymologists credit the Dutch word *"kolf"* later translated *"gouf"* by the Scots. The word, by the way means *club*, (as in the stick used to play the game; not the watering hole at the end of the 18th hole).

Great Scott!

If the expression *Great Scott!* sounds a bit pompous, well, there's good reason.

And if you don't know which Scott it is that's so great, take a note!

Great Scott refers to one Winfred Scott, commander in the Mexican War and the Whig party's nomination for president in the election of 1852.

Scott was known for being stuck on himself. And as a result, his campaign was likewise marked with pride and arrogance. Still and so, he campaigned with great fervency. But his opposition dubbed him *"Great Scott!"* mocking his pomposity.

As a result, the phrase is a pretentious reference today. (And for what it's worth, Great Scott was defeated by Franklin Pierce... which just goes to show!)

High on the Hog

O.K. Pig Anatomy 101.

Things *high on the hog* include your basic pork favorites: tenderloin, bacon, pork chops, spare ribs and holiday hams. (In other words, the better pig parts we've grown to know and love, especially here in the South!)

For what it's worth, there were *low* hog parts too (including but not limited to -- pigs feet, knuckles, jowls... oh, and don't forget those chitlins)!

Pretty self explanatory when you reflect upon how food was once allocated back on plantations of old. (Those in the big house ate high; while the slaves ate low. Are you getting the picture here?)

It's an expression that speaks for itself!

Hobnob

Deriving from the Old English, *hobnob* literally translates: "have and have not," or "to give and take." And in taverns of old, that's exactly what transpired!

From the land famous for its pub crawls, our British cousins are renowned for socializing in local pubs, where pals were quick to offer a toast on behalf of their closest friends.

As one had to give, and another receive, *hob-nobbing* was quite the social event of the day.

And as drinks were bought in rounds (see freeloader, page 42), the word *hobnob* had as much to do with the giving and taking of information as it did with the giving and taking of ale!

Hocus Pocus

While yes, there is a similar sounding phrase uttered in Roman Catholic mass (*"Hoc est (enim) corpus"* meaning "This is my body") there's no real evidence that this same phrase has anything at all to do with the expression magicians use just before they saw a woman in half.

Most likely, *hocus pocus* is nothing more than a reduplication (fancy word meaning the second word rhymes with the root word. Think *hoity-toity*. Think *hanky-panky*... Just don't think too long!)

What we *do* know, is that this fun expression traces back to early jugglers and stage performers of the 17th century and was used for all things magic or deception.

Since that time, it has been contracted into a much more familiar word -- namely, hoax.

Hook, Line & Sinker

This one describes one really gullible dude -- you know... the guy who swallows your story *hook, line and sinker!*

The comparison is to that of one eager fish -- so hungry for bait, that he chomps beyond the hook, gobbling up *hook, line and sinker* as well.

Now folklore credits this expression to Davy Crockett, whose tall tales of conquering big bears with bare hands became a beloved part of American folklore.

Previous expressions, similar in nature, however, trace this one back to our British cousins, for whom swallowing a gudgeon (a form of bait fish, much akin to a minnow) predates our own version of the phrase.

Influenza

Who knew that the common flu could possess such superstitious origins?

Well, believe it or not, it's true!

Our naming of this common epidemic (long version best pronounced with an Italian accent) *influenza* goes back to the mid 1700s when the first outbreak of the dreaded virus was recorded in Rome.

Belief at the time held that the stars and planets influenced our life events, including such evil and contagious epidemics as the flu.

From this, *influenza* (the Italian word for influence) became the given name for the bug that still makes our evening news every winter season!

In the Bag

The oldest reference to *in the bag* is said to have come from hunting lingo, with the "bag" being that used to bag game.

But the more colorful explanation has to do with cock fighting (that illegal competition between gamecocks -- fitted with spurs -- and fighting to the death, in what has to be one of the most gruesome betting sports around).

As prize gamecocks were secretly toted in cloth bags, "cocky" bird owners made the phrase their own as they boasted "This one's *in the bag!*" (meaning the bookies were counting on victory even prior to the fight taking place).

In the Doghouse

Not to be confused with Fido's doghouse, the background behind this dog-of-an-expression is rather historic, though not too pleasant. Its origin traces to the first slaves brought to America.

To be clear, when you're *in the doghouse*, you're in a place you don't want to be. The reason is less about being in trouble and more about being out of luck. Here's the story:

On the decks of early slave ships were small cubicles, referred to as doghouses (owing to their size and unappealing nature).

Sailors in charge of these slaves were said to be on *"doghouse duty,"* keeping watch of an unappealing situation, often in unappealing weather. All the while the rest of the crew stayed below the decks, out of harm's way.

In the Hole

To be *in the hole*, as you might imagine, refers to being in debt. And yes, the expression originated in gambling houses of old.

With poker the preferred game of the mid 1800s, it was during poker's heyday that gambling houses flourished.

As games were played and bets were lost, cash was constantly stuffed into the slot or hole in the center of the gaming table. The money collected was held in a box underneath this hole, which, of course, was never to be seen again by the gambling patron.

Those who wound up with more money in this hole than in their pockets were said to be *in the hole*. Thus, the association of being cashless with the expression has remained ever since.

A fairly recent addition to our language, the first mention of anything *jumbo* was in reference to an elephant purchased by P.T. Barnum in 1881.

Historians tell us that Jumbo was captured in West Africa in 1869 and was at the time, touted as the largest elephant known to man.

Weighing in at six-and-a-half tons, Jumbo was a hit at the London Zoological Society, which is precisely where P.T. found him.

Barnum was reported to have paid $30,000 for Jumbo. It was said he recouped his investment ten-fold within six weeks.

Thanks to Jumbo's size and P.T.'s savvy marketing skills, Jumbo became *the* word for the biggest thing going even today!

Jump the Gun

Jumping the gun means you made a sudden move or decision without really giving it much thought. And if you ask the hunters in your midst where this phrase comes from, they'll take the credit, saying *jumping the gun* refers to game that takes flight just before the shoot.

But this would be wrong.

The original gun jumper was an enthusiastic runner (more specifically, a sprinter), so eager to win the race that he jumped ahead of the starting shot.

And it is that very same notion of jumping ahead of the game that gives us our gun-jumping meaning we hold for the phrase today.

Kick the Bucket

In case you aren't familiar with this one, to *kick the bucket* means you died. You croaked. That's it. You're done.

And to be clear, the expression has nothing to do with kicking a pail out from under a man being hanged.

No. No. Nay. Nay.

Instead, the phrase originates in the slaughterhouses of old, where hogs were slashed and hung (by their heels, no less) and strung by a pulley across a wooden block called a *bucket*. (Imagine the hog, hoisted from a rope and pulley much akin to those used to lower buckets into wells, and you start to get the gruesome picture.)

In its struggle to survive, the struggling, slaughtered hog *kicks the bucket* just before giving up the ghost.

Kid Gloves

No. This isn't something your children wear in the winter months. Instead, the phrase is short for *kidding gloves*.

The first *kid gloves* were designed for the well-to-do in 14th century England. As workers of the day needed work gloves to protect their hands, they found these pretentious, finger less, non-practical gloves of the hoity-toity to be a joke, and thus referred to them as fake, or *kidding gloves*.

To treat someone with *kid gloves* was a further mockery of the upper class, as by all means, they would never have a need for gloves other than to show their social status. As a result, we today use the phrase to connote treating someone pretentiously special.

Kit and Caboodle

So the question is, "What's a *caboodle*?"

(Fortunately we've got boodles of answers!)

The word *boedel* is a Dutch word meaning "belongings" or "effects"(in other words, the stuff you think you own.)

Curiously, common thieves gave us this one, referring to their take from a burglary as their "boodle." (FYI, this is the same base word that pirates used in reference to the "booty" they stole from ships at sea. So now we have thieves *and* pirates to thank.)

As burglars carried their tools in *kits*, a clean sweep of a house meant you got away with *the kit and the boodle*. In time this evolved into our everyday: *kit and caboodle*, which means the entire lot of things.

Knock on Wood

So what about knocking on wood makes for good luck? A superstition that pre-dates Christianity, certain pagan beliefs held that good spirits resided in trees. Thus, to knock on a tree was to call upon those spirits to protect you as you journeyed through the forest.

Later Christianity adapted its own version of touching wood, in reverence of the crucifixion, making wood and certain rosary beads the token touchstone for the same expression.

So common is the reference that some even credit this time honored superstition as the basis for why touching the home base of a tree makes you safe from capture in the childhood game of hide-and-seek.

Know 'Um Like a Book

Know a person like a book and you know that person about as well as a person can be known! But interestingly enough, the expression traces back to the days when there weren't a lot of books to be had... when memorizing was the only way to go.

Before printing presses made everyday items out of Bibles (and later, other books as well), those with access to original texts had to memorize scripture and passages to keep the stories alive.

Monks were the first to master this concept, as memorizing sacred texts cover to cover, (or scroll to scroll as the case was then), meant you had to know it through and through.

So too, when someone knows you like a book, they know you pretty darned well.

Knuckle Down

Not to be confused with *knuckling under*, (which sadly, means you've been defeated) *knuckling down* means you're getting down to brass tacks... (Oh wait! That's another story entirely.)

One story traces the expression to a time when knuckles included *all* bodily joints, (not just finger joints). As the spine would be our largest assembly of knuckles, *knuckling down* meant, in some contexts, putting one's back into the task at hand.

But the other, more likely explanation dates back to 17th century England, wherein the game of marbles, (quite the popular children's sport) had rules requiring each player to shoot from outside the ring of play, making *knuckling down* synonymous with any focused attention to the game at hand.

Lame Duck

A quacky title for sure, but just so you know, the first *lame duck* wasn't daffy. Instead it was a member of the British Stock Exchange who couldn't meet his liabilities come settlement time, and thus flew off without settling his account.

From this we applied the term to our politicos who, by way of losing an election, can no longer return to their flock, even though their own party has been retained.

Like the wounded bird for which it is named, a *lame duck* becomes the responsibility of the new administration, and is often appointed to some office that requires no election, just to keep him busy until he can limp his way out of office.

Letting the Cat Out of the Bag

Letting the Cat Out of the Bag means you squealed! (In short, it means you revealed a secret before it was meant to be known.)

Ironically, the origin of this phrase has to do with squealing as well (only in this case, we mean it literally).

Tracing back to the Middle Ages when the Muslims invaded Europe, pork was declared unclean, and thus, forbidden by law.

As a result, pigs were sold undercover in cloth bags known as pokes (which also gives us our phrase, *Pig in a Poke,* but I digress...).

But when on occasion, a cat was substituted for the more expensive pig, it wasn't until the customer got home and *let the cat out of the bag* that the secret was revealed!

Lewd

Most often used in a triad (as in lewd, crude and socially unacceptable), the word *lewd* as we use it today suggests a person of loose moral values. But in its earliest context, this was not the case at all.

A derivative of the Old English word "loewed," the original word *lewd* was simply a label for an everyday lay person (i.e., a person not trained, nor ordained in the clergy).

A reference to the commoner (one ignorant and lacking cultivation), in time lewd's meaning became synonymous with vulgar (another word that originally meant common or base).

All from a simple attempt to separate the commoners from the clergy, *lewd* has since evolved into a label for all things promiscuous, unchaste and morally corrupt.

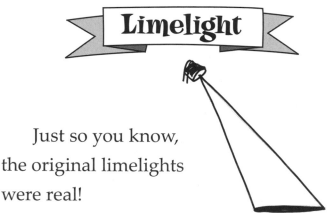

Limelight

Just so you know,
the original limelights
were real!

Early stage lighting (and get this: the
same light used for lighthouses) was made of
lime (otherwise known as calcium oxide).

Created by crossing a stream of oxygen
with a stream of hydrogen, all while burning
the two on a lime surface, the combination
yielded a brilliant white light, still used in
theatrical settings today.

From this came our present day notion
of being in the spotlight, which was precisely
what limelight did for those back in the early
days of theater.

Lion's Share

Take the *lion's share*, and you're taking more than your fair part. The expression comes to us compliments of Aesop's Fables (a story with a moral, often using animals... in this case, a lion, a fox, a jackal and a wolf).

As the animals return from a day's hunt, the lion asks the jackal to quarter the spoils of the stag they have nabbed. No sooner does he divide things into fourths, does the lion begin to argue that he is due a greater percentage.

Specifically, he requests one quarter for himself, another for his family, another simply for his bravery.

The fourth part he offers "to him who would dare lay a paw on it."

The fox grumbles as he departs,
"You may share the labors of the great,
but you will not share the spoil."

Lollypop

The original candy-on-a-stick, *lollypops* trace to the late 1700s. The first reference was to a soft candy product, not the hard sucrose we know it as today.

Word enthusiasts credit the combination of two words: *lolly* (tongue) and *pop* (slap). Its roots trace to Romani origins (i.e. gypsy tribes hailing from Central and Eastern Europe).

Named for the sound it made when slurped, the *lollypop* was an immediate hit.

By the Roaring 20s the *lollypop* made its way to America. (And within a decade, the Tootsie Pop was born!)

The concept was a novel one: candy on a stick that pops in and out of your mouth. In Europe they're still lollies.

(But here we call ours suckers!)

Loophole

A word that is today synonymous with a little opening to get you out of a tight squeeze, who knew the original loophole was a castle feature, architectural in origin? Well, it was!

In castles of old, loopholes were those narrow window like slits, crafted into the walls themselves, as a form of security.

These small openings, spaced every few feet apart, were designed both for observation as well as for shooting arrows. And while these holes were small and narrow, if need be, they could also serve as an emergency escape should the castle be taken under attack.

From this do we derive our current definition of a *loophole* today, as an undetected way out of a problem on the rise.

Mad as a March Hare

O.K. So let's not confuse our writers here... For while Lewis Carroll *did* give life to the character, *Mad as a March Hare* (the expression) goes as far back as Chaucer.

Now some will tell you the original was *Mad as Marsh Hare*, but regardless... both marsh and March involve rabbits, and (worse), their mating habits in the spring.

(File this under: more info than we ever wanted to know, but... O.K. Here we go!)

In breeding season, the buck hare has long been noted for his crazy antics, credited to the change of seasons... (Yeah. Right. Whatever.)

We're told that with the onset of spring the buck hare frolics in ways that appear... well, insane to one observing his habits. (Are you starting to note a lunar-tic theme here?)

No matter...

From this, the expression was born! (And for the record, *mad* means crazy, not angry.)

72

Make No Bones About It!

Think comfy, country... Think "House on the Prairie" times of old when cooking was done in a great big pot over a loving, open hearth, and you start to understand *making no bones about it.*

Sweet as it was, it was also a time when it was not uncommon to find all sorts of things floating about in that one big pot.

As scraps of meat were tossed in, small bones were pretty much inevitable. And as a result, it required a degree of caution as you ate, seeing as you might run across a bone in your stew.

Now your more particular guests might've complained about the bones in their bowls, but those who just appreciated the meal, making no big deal of the occasional inconvenience, were said to have *made no bones about it.*

Making Your Mark

Most everyone you meet wants to make a mark in this world...

It's an expression that means you've arrived!

But at one point, *making your mark* simply meant your work was distinguishable from someone else's.

Once upon a time it was the practice of smiths and artisans to mark their wares with a symbol or a logo placed somewhere on their art.

Once that mark was known, the artist (having *made his mark* in the world) became the symbol of all things successful.

Maverick

It's a word that today, stands for all things unique, individualistic and independent.

Its legacy comes from Texas, when, in the mid 1800s, cattle branding was *the* way to identify your cattle from everyone else's.

Along comes Samuel Maverick, owner of one of the largest ranches around, who decides that in *not* branding his cattle, he could efficiently identify his own.

As a result, Maverick declared that any cattle found without a brand was his and his alone. As this method would've included all wild and unclaimed beasts as well, his attempts failed. (Nice try, but it didn't work.)

However, in time his name became synonymous with anything that hadn't been claimed by a prior group.

Mind Your P's and Q's

One of our more colorful expressions, *Mind Your P's and Q's,* has at least two stories vying for its origin. One involves early printing presses and moveable type, wherein letters cast were the mirror opposite of what they would be on the page. (As P's and Q's were easily confused, minding them meant you paid close attention to the smallest of details.)

The more popular story, however, credits English taverns of old wherein it was the bartender's job to keep up with the consumption of his beer-drinking patrons.

Marking P's and Q's on a small slate board behind the bar, the barkeep could mind the pints and quarts of his customer, both for tab-paying purposes as well as for intoxication purposes. (Think British version of *Don't Drink and Drive!*)

Name is Mud

To give credit where credit is due, the expression synonymous with one lousy reputation, was in use long before Abraham Lincoln's assassination ("mud" being Old English slang for "fool").

But it is true the phrase took on new meaning when Dr. Samuel Mudd lost his own good name for setting the broken leg of John Wilkes Booth.

While Mudd was sentenced to a life in prison for his deed (and thought by some to be a co-conspirator), this same Dr. Mudd later gained notoriety for contributions that helped curtail the outbreak of yellow fever in the prison hospital.

Just another reason we can't peg this one directly to the man. But we can thank Mudd's adherence to his profession's code of ethics for putting new life into a phrase that today, makes those historic details a lot more fun to memorize!

Nepotism

A fancy word meaning you hired your nephew, *nepotism* means you showed favoritism in hiring a relative when some-one else might've been more qualified for the job.

First coined during the reign of Pope Alexander VI, *nepotism* sadly became an all too familiar term when certain bishops and popes, having no children of their own, gave preferential treatment to their nephews for appointments within the church's hierarchy.

From the Latin word "nepos" (meaning nephew or grandson) *nepotism* in a business context covers any family member shown favoritism strictly on the basis of kinship.

(In other words: it's all relative!)

Nest Egg

Believe it or not, the whole *nest egg* concept (which today refers to any informal way of stashing away cash) has been with us since the 17th century.

The first *nest eggs* were man-made.

They eggs made out of clay, and placed in the hen's nest to inspire that hen to lay more eggs! (Today farmers just leave one real egg for the same effect.)

In time the same notion was applied to human habits for saving money, with the *nest egg* representing that stash of savings, set aside in efforts to motivate a person to lay aside more! (In other words, when it comes to savings, sometimes we've gotta *egg* you on!)

Nickname

Gotta love this one... Who knew? Those *nicknames* (or fun names) we call our pals just for grins... well they've been around since the 14th century!

But why *nickname*?

Well, believe it or not, this one's another mispronunciation that, over time, we've managed to slur into a word all our own!

Originally pronounced "ekename" (*eke* being an Old English word for "extra"), this *nickname* made sense by definition as many folks were called by one name even though they had another, far more fancy on their birth certificates.

But regardless, since we aren't too formal particularly here in the South, over time, *nick-name* is the *ekename* that stuck!

(In the) Nick of Time

There once was a time when tally sticks were nicked to keep a count for any number of various sporting events in need of a tab.

This nicking system was invented when certain games required a score keeping mechanism fair to all.

Who knew this same system would become a practical tool in both early churches as well as in British Parliament for keeping up with attendance?

The trick was to arrive before the count got to your seat, which meant you arrived in the *nick of time.* This also gives us the meaning we hold for the expression today. (It means you got there just under the wire.)

Nightmare

Not your basic female horse, this mare (nightmare) describes an evil spirit.

Taken from the Old English word "maere" the first nightmare was a more like a goblin (for lack of a better word) believed to disturb a person's sleep by sitting on the chest of the sleeper, causing a feeling of suffocation and terror in the night.

Over time *nightmares* became the word describing both the spirit and the feeling it produced.

Today nightmares include everything from scary dreams to experiences that startle you while you sleep.

(Boo!)

(For more on goblins see page 45.)

Nincompoop

In case you don't know, a *nincompoop* is a dunce, an idiot... a stupid person.

And some historians will tell you the word was born of the Latin phrase *"non compos mentis,"* which translates: *"without ability"* or *"of unsound mind."*

No doubt, it works. (Though certain sources poo-poo the notion that it ever started out as anything Latin, thus so academic.)

But even more interesting than this word's origin, is a recent statistic citing a survey of some 2,000 Brits, wherein the word *nincompoop* was voted the nation's favorite word out of some 16,000 words!

(Even for us *nincompoops*, that's a pretty impressive statistic! Gotta love those Brits for spotting a word that's just plain fun to say!)

Nip it in the Bud

Gardeners among us get this one, as some plants will grow like crazy if left uncontrolled. Pruning is the key (both to plants and to this expression) as horticulturists have known for centuries that nipping the bud of a plant prevents it from reproducing fruit.

Likewise, good gardeners know that to ensure larger blossoms or fruit, *nipping it in the bud* will direct all a plant's resources to those blooms that remain.

Gardener or not, the expression today is synonymous with "instantly ending a project before it grows out of control."

This works for plants as well as plans for when left to their own devices, both grow wildly out of control if someone doesn't *nip 'em in the bud!*

84

Nitwit

Nitwit -- meaning a person of little to no intelligence -- is an American favorite, though we can't really take credit for its origin.

A combination of two words: one English / one German, the *nit* we take from the German word *nicht*, meaning "without." Add that to our English word, *wit*, meaning "intelligence" or "an ability to comprehend" and you have one "without ability" (or in other words, a person without any sense at all)!

These are the sorts of words you get when cultures cross pollinate.

(Fun, huh?)

Not Worth His Salt

A person *not worth his salt* is one not worth the money he earns. And conversely, someone said to be *salt of the earth*, is about as solid a person as you'll ever meet.

So as you've probably guessed by now, this means *salt* held some value somewhere along the way. And there's a good reason for that!

In days of old, Roman officers gave salt rations to their soldiers and civil servants, thanks to the preservative qualities that were of great value, pre-refrigeration.

Interestingly enough, salt today (*sal* in Latin), shares the same root for our monied word, salary (from the Latin, *salarium*).

Building upon the same notion, the English phrase *true to his salt*, was the ultimate compliment, describing one faithful to his employer.

Odds and Ends

As an expression, *odds and ends* can mean any number of sordid things. To be sure, *odds and ends* are random elements -- bits and pieces (or bits and bobs if you're British) -- in other words, leftover items, ranging from cloth to building materials.

History traces the first *odds and ends* to lumber yards of old, where *odds* consisted of those pieces of board split irregularly by the sawmill (oddly shaped), and *ends* were those leftover ends of a plank too short to sell for anything useful.

In psychological terms, to *be* at *odds and ends* means you're in a state of disarray -- scattered and feeling good for nothing.

Much akin to the expression, *to be at loose ends,* to be at *odds and ends* means you're likewise a bit frazzled.

Off Color

Jokes said to be *off color*, are jokes that are dirty, tacky or in some way lacking in taste. And while several stories exist for the origin of this phrase, one of the more popular ones has to do with the early years of nightclubs, where colored spotlights directed the audience's attention on the featured performer.

As hosts and emcees were often known to work their material in between acts, some were known to use less than clean humor, stepping side of center stage to dodge the spotlight (just in case the audience took offense).

By this, *off color* became synonymous with the risque language or performance we equate with the expression today.

Off-the-Cuff

An *off-the-cuff* comment is something that comes with no advanced planning or preparation. Speak *off-the-cuff* and you're speaking extemporaneously -- (big word meaning without a lot of forethought).

But the background of the expression is far less literary -- far more literal in its origin.

Working *off-the-cuff* goes back to the pubs of Old England where bartenders, dressed in starched white shirts, were often known to keep up with the bar tabs of their customers by writing on the cuffs of their shirtsleeves.

Come time to clear that tab, quick bartenders could tally the total, right *off-the-cuff*, which means, he didn't have to over think it: he just went with what he had.

O.K.

Word enthusiasts have a ball with this one! One story traces the origin of *O.K.* all the way back to the Greek, *ola kala*, meaning "It is good," which works for me, but political buffs will tell you, "No. No. Nay. Nay!"

Instead they insist this simple phrase means "Everything's all right!" And it comes to us compliments of Martin Van Buren and his 1840 re-election run for the presidency.

To be clear, it was "The Democratic O.K. Club" -- (named for Old Kinderhook -- Van Buren's nickname, based on his boyhood hometown of Kinderhook, NY.) -- that really popularized the phrase in America.

Ever since, *O.K.* became everyday lingo; its meaning synonymous with "alright," which is, of course, precisely what those two little letters still represent today!

One Fell Swoop

So what's a swoop, and why did it fall? Well, first of all, it didn't.

The *fell* we reference in context of this expression, has nothing to do with falling, (or failing, as it is often misspelled and mispronounced, especially here in the South).

Nope. The basis for this one is a word that means "cruel" or "mean." (Think *felon*, and you start to get the idea.)

In its original context, *one fell swoop* was coined to describe one mean or cruel bird of prey, swooping down to attack its victim.

That same dive-bomb approach we've since borrowed to describe any other ruthlessly fierce (if not deadly) situation.

On the Nose

To *win* by a nose takes us back to the early days of horse racing, but to *BE on the nose*, puts you in a different setting entirely: namely, radio studios of old.

As our first radio broadcasts were staged live in a studio, with the director across the way in a sound-proof booth, hand signals were critical in timing the show's elements.

In the same way that sawing hand to neck meant "Cut!" so too, did the hand sign for cuing out on time come to be finger to nose.

From this, today's phrase *on the nose* became synonymous for anything timing out perfectly.

On the Wagon

Yes, we've all heard it! To be *on the wagon*, means you've gone dry, as in no alcohol, which begs the question, who's wagon was it and why was it dry?

The original wagon on which reformed alcoholics pledged to stay, was a horse-drawn water cart of the late 1800s.

In the heyday of Prohibition, many a reformer would take a vow to stop drinking alcohol, substituting only water for liquid refreshment. The backslider to the vow, was said to have fallen off the water wagon and back onto hard liquor or moonshine.

Pay Dirt

Pay dirt is an expression that means profit or success, usually entered into rather quickly (as in "When Bubba won the lottery, he hit *pay dirt!*")

But *pay dirt* as an expression has a history that was quite literal in the early on.

Comprised of two words -- pay and dirt -- the expression dates as far back as the mid 1850s, and pertains to...?

Think gold rush. Think mining. Think of those who scurried out west exchanging life and family for one good swing of a pick ax.

So go the colorful beginnings of hitting *pay dirt* -- an idiom that is as literal as it is colorful, originating with the California gold rush.

Poor as a Church Mouse

Poor as a church mouse traces back to 17th century England, though some claim the expression finds its roots in German and French expressions recorded much earlier.

To grasp the concept, keep in mind that our modern day churches (with facilities like fellowship halls and church libraries) are a far cry from the structures of old, used solely for worship services and prayers.

As the village church (central to the layout of most new towns), was one of the few structures that had neither food, nor running water on hand (much less the facilities for which to prepare a meal), to be *poor as a church mouse* meant you not only had nothing, you had nothing of worth to attract so much as a mouse.

POSH

Some say POSH is an acronym for Port Out / Starboard Home. And the Peninsular & Oriental Steam Navigation Company takes credit for the story, as its vessels were said to be the first to carry passengers and mail between England and India.

As port side cabins received the early morning sun, they were much to be preferred (as passengers then had the rest of the day to cool down).

Starboard cabins on the other hand, got the afternoon rays (making them toasty by nightfall).

Per this logic, the opposite would be the case coming home, meaning the more desirable (shaded) cabins were always on reserve for VIPs and elite travelers.

To this end, port (left side) out, starboard (right side) home, made up the acronym POSH, though the theory is one etymologists still debate today.

Pot Luck

If it sounds familiar it is. The pot in *pot luck* is the same pot referenced in *gone to pot*, which is to say, that black kettle hanging over an open fire in most every medieval household. (In Ireland, the same was called the *pot of hospitality*, as it was constantly simmering, inviting hungry guests to partake.)

From the French *pot-au-feu* (meaning: fire pot), this constant companion of the hard working peasant provided plain and simple food consisting of nothing more than broth and leftovers from prior meals.

Whether lucky by way of the food you might find (a scrap of meat here, a bit of potato there), or lucky by way of amount there was to serve, *pot luck* meant whatever's in the pot, you were lucky to get, regardless its contents, or how far that stew would stretch!

97

Pot Shot

The original expression *"A shot for the pot"* was a hunter's term, meaning game that was hunted would later be cooked in the big pot for all to share.

As sustenance was the goal, there were no rules for this kind of hunting, so shooting from any distance, no matter how close, was not only fair game, it made life easier.

The expression was first recorded in the late 1700s when, by both military and civilian standards, *pot shots* became synonymous with shooting anything within reach.

In time, the inference shifted from shooting lingo, to encompass verbal *pot shots* as well (meaning the person receiving the jab was an easy target, given no chance to defend himself or exit an awkward situation).

Powwow

Today's *powwow* suggests a meeting in which there is more talk than results, and more often than not, the word is referenced in political context when used today.

As you might've picked up from the sound of the word, *powwow* comes to us compliments of our Native American Indian ancestry, and depicts those public feasts, dances and gatherings that brought tribes together.

Today the expression is more commonly used in political circles to signify any uproarious meeting at which there is more noise than deliberation.

Yet, while we use the term loosely to describe such, we must keep in mind that the original *powwows* were noisy because they took place after success in war or in hunting.

Quagmire

In nature, a *quagmire* is a swamp or bog -- (in other words, a place that gives way when you step on it).

As a figure of speech, the concept is much the same when you stop to consider that when you're IN a *quagmire*, you're all but stuck in the mud!

Linguistically speaking, *quagmire* is a combination of two words: *quag* coming from the Old English *cwabba* (meaning to shake or tremble); *mire* being a marsh, or muddy, soft spot of land. Put the two together and you have yourself one sticky situation, indeed.

The word dates back to the mid 1500s and was coined to describe ground that appeared solid, but in reality was unstable. Today we use the same to describe any similar feeling of uncertainty, or a sense of being bogged down.

Quarantine

The notion of *quarantine* goes back as far as 400 AD, but to give credit where credit is due, it was in Venice, Italy where the notion of *quarantine* first gained notoriety.

In 1403, Venice established the first maritime *quarantine* to protect locals from the black plague, requiring all ships to dock in port for 40 days. From this, *quarantine* has become synonymous with all things isolated or restricted.

As with *quadrant* and *quartet*, quarantine's *quar* prefix hails from the Italian root word, *quaranta*, meaning *forty*.

This 40-day isolation period was designed in effort to prevent the spread of plagues and various diseases, though today it has come to mean any detention or isolation period designed to protect humans from something harmful, dangerous or contagious.

Reimburse

Reimburse someone and you've paid back what you owe. In other words, you have made restoration by *repaying* the exact sum of money you borrowed.

But the part you might NOT know is just how literal the translation is.

Derived from three Latin words, "re" (meaning *back,*) "im" (meaning *in*) and "bursa" (which was the Latin word for *purse*) *reimburse*, as we use the word today, meant quite literally, that you put the money back into another's purse.

(If only they were all this easy!)

Riding Roughshod

Ride roughshod, and you've acted in a way that showed little to no regard for the other person. Likewise, the *roughshod* horse (from which the phrase derives) had just as little concern as by definition, *roughshod* horses were those with nails protruding from their shoes.

The notion was noble enough -- try to keep your horse from slipping, especially while in battle.

But once on the battlefield, it was soon determined that *roughshod* horses not only held a better grip, they could also do serious damage to any enemy that might have fallen in the fight.

(If you're not eating right now, try to imagine the gory scene of one trampled by a *roughshod* horse! That same image gives us our meaning of "treating someone brutally," which we associate with *roughshod* today.)

Rings True

No sooner did we come up with the brilliant idea of gold and silver coins, did some counterfeiter come up with the notion of counterfeit money. As a result, someone, somewhere had to devise a way to tell the difference!

At one point the only sure fire way to know for certain if your coin was real was to drop it and listen for the tone it produced. It was said that solid coins would *ring true*, while counterfeit coins (i.e., those filled with nickel or copper) fell flat.

The test was called ringing a coin, and it was later determined to be less than reliable. But regardless, the practice gave us our phrase *rings true* connoting something that proves to be accurate.

Ritzy

When a person's name earns him a word all his own, then it stands to reason that this is one impressive person!

Such is true of Caesar Ritz, the Swiss restaurateur and hotel magnate, who built the famous Ritz Hotel in Paris in 1898.

Known for the strictest standards of excellence, Ritz earned the reputation of being the greatest hotelier in all of the Western World.

Once Ritz Hotels were established in London, New York and a handful of other prestigious cities, having anything like the Ritz made it *ritzy*, and thus became the standard for anything posh, extravagant or lavish.

Rule of Thumb

Rule of thumb has more than one origin. (Seems lots of cultures want to take credit for this one!)

One source cites *rule of thumb* as a rough measure (the length between the last knuckle and thumb tip being roughly an inch). Such was the solution for early merchants selling ribbon, lace or cloth, when a more accurate measuring device wasn't readily available.

Another *rule of thumb* dates to a reference in English Common Law wherein a married woman, considered the property of her husband, could not be whipped by anything thicker than the width of her husband's thumb.

Either way *rule of thumb* is a non-official measure (as opposed to something linear, logical or otherwise precise).

Rule the Roost

Granted, the cocky way of a barnyard rooster certainly would fit the description of one who *rules the roost*, but according to our sources this phrase is believed to reference something entirely different.

If you can believe it, the original was not *rule the roost*, but *rule the roast!*

(Who knew?)

The expression seems to have come from 15th century England where it was made in reference to the master of the house, seated at the head of his table as he served his guests.

Being responsible for both family and servants, this "roast ruler" was both head of his table and head of his household, which gives us our "person in charge" meaning today.

(Technically, I think we can thank William Shakespeare, who made popular the *Rule the Roast* version in his play Henry VI.)

Sabotage

Who knew a simple little shoe could bring on such a ruckus? Who knew a French *sabot* (meaning shoe) could make for *saboteurs*!

Sabotage suggests a deliberate destruction or delay. And the origin of the word came about when little *sabots* gave way to the more serious word we use today.

With the introduction of weaving looms came protests by French peasants losing their jobs to machinery. As the story goes, it was the jamming of their wooden shoes into these looms that brought about the first *sabotage*.

The word gained renewed popularity after WWI when it referenced the destruction of enemy bridges, railroads and machinery.

From this, came our sophisticated word -- *sabotage*.

('*Wooden shoe*' just know it?)

108

Scot Free

Scot free has nothing to do with Scotland, the Scottish people or even Scotch Tape.

Instead, it's a word that comes to us compliments of the Anglo-Saxon word *sceot*, which was in its original context, a tax or a fine.

In case you don't know, *scot free* means you got away without paying. And the most common use of the word dates back to Old England where a *"scot and lot"* was a levy placed on all subjects according to their ability to pay.

Now technically today we might call this an income tax. But regardless, the expression, *scot free,* means you got away without paying (tax wise or otherwise)!

Seventh Heaven

A place beyond description, it is said that those who make it to this level of bliss will forever chant the praises of Allah. It is from the Islamic faith that we derive the phrase *seventh heaven*.

The Islamic faith holds that there are seven levels of heaven, each progressively better than the previous one... each requiring a purer life to attain.

According to Mohammed, the *seventh heaven* is formed of *"...divine light beyond the power of the tongue to describe."* And it is only in this *seventh heaven* that pure bliss is attained (as according to the faith) this is where God himself resides with his angels.

Shoddy

As we use the word today, *shoddy* has come to represent any product or project that is inferior in quality. Though in the early on, *shoddy* was a technical term used to describe a by-product that came from manufacturing wool.

In woolen terms *shod* referred to the fluff part of combed wool that was thrown off in the spinning. While this fluff was still used to make new wool, it was short-stapled, which meant the clothes made from it did not last as long.

As that fabric was inferior to the long-stapled or combing wools, it became known as *shoddy*... hence our reference today.

"Baaaaad Wool"

Silhouette

We can thank Etienne de Silhouette, Comptroller General of France in 1759, for these black on white pictures named in his honor.

Under Silhouette's administration, businesses were ordered, in the name of savings, to do away with any and all unnecessary details.

By the same rule, even paintings were reduced to mere outlines. As a result, black on white portraits became popular and were called *silhouettes* in honor of the financier whose economic plan had suggested them.

Skeletons
in the
Closet

Back in the dark ages it was a long held superstition that a doctor could not cut into the body of a dead person for fear he might disturb the ghost of the deceased.

As you might imagine, this made the study of human anatomy all but impossible. As a result, cadavers became hot items on the black market for doctors seriously interested in understanding the inner workings of the human body.

When grave robbers began supplying the goods in the dark of night, many a good doctor became suspect for having a *skeleton in his closet*, which gives us today's meaning of something hidden or secret.

Slapstick

Yep. There actually *is* a device called a *slapstick*, and as you might imagine, it began with the vaudeville comedian.

If you must know, a *slapstick* was made by fastening two flat pieces of wood together on one end leaving the other end loose to make an extra loud *clack*.

When used by an actor to hit another person, the *slapstick* amplified the effect, and thus, produced laughter when used in the context of the show.

In its day, the *slapstick* was a noun, which is to say, an actual prop. Today the reference is more often used as an adjective to describe the zany kind of horseplay synonymous with the original sticks.

Slush Fund

An expression associated with excess funds in a campaign or business, today's *slush fund* suggests something unofficial and often slightly shady (i.e., off the books).

Instead, the first *slush fund* was literal.

And it was nautical.

Slush was what sailors called surplus fat or grease collected from the foods they fried while out at sea. Crews commonly sold or traded their grease in port, pooling their funds from this slush to buy personal items like soap or razors.

Today the term is used in business or politics when referencing unofficial funds set aside to help keep a business afloat. (But the connotation is not always above board, like it was aboard the ships that gave us the story).

Snob

While one story has it that *snob* is a variation on the Scottish word, *snab* (a word meaning, *shoemaker*), the more colorful story (and the one I prefer) traces our first snobs to Oxford and Cambridge, for you see, the earliest colleges were never designed for the common man.

Instead, they were made for nobility -- those who would need an education to lead a country.

But when Cambridge decided to open its doors to more than just royalty, entering students had to register as either "nobilitate" or "sine nobilitate" (without nobility).

The latter was shortened to "S. nob" and this is where we get our word *snob* today.

Son of a Gun

Son of a gun is also nautical in origin. The expression traces back to the early days of the British Navy when women were allowed to accompany their men at sea.

One version has it that pregnancies on board made for little privacy come time to birth those babies, thus it became common practice for women to give birth beneath the ship's guns.

Another take on the same suggests that when births occurred with no clue as to who the father was, the ship's captain would log the child under: *son of a gun*.

With this, *son of a gun* osmosed into a reference to one conceived illegitimately, thus making a euphemistic pun out of the more vulgar reference to a *"son of a ...."*

Southpaw

The first *southpaws* were left-handed baseball pitchers. But today the term is synonymous with any left-handed person. Baseball or no, the story is still a great one.

Before nighttime baseball, the first ball games were played in the light of day (and in the heat of the sun).

Major league diamonds were, as a rule, laid out so that the batter would face east, opposite the setting sun, to spare his eyes the glare.

Because of this configuration, the pitcher faced west, with his right hand to the north and his left to the south. From this early baseball layout we coined the term *southpaw* for any left-handed pitcher.

Speakeasy

The Irish are to thank for this word, as it had to do with their prohibition laws of long ago.

According to such laws, one was not allowed to raise his voice riotously or start a brawl in any establishment where liquor was sold. To do so might bring to the attention of police, the existence of the illegal establishment.

The result was that patrons were to *speak easy*, both in the joint, as well as about the joint!

Today's *speakeasies* are simply places where illegal alcohol is sold!

Spittin' Image

The story behind this phrase is that the phrase is a corruption of a soulful, more spiritual expression: *spirit and image*.

Historical context suggests the phrase was coined by our African American ancestry, to describe a relative (usually a child) who both looked like and had the disposition of another family member (usually a mother or a father).

Spirit and image was used so regularly in the South that over time it was phonetically contracted to *spittin' image*.

The expression today still carries the old meaning of one being just like another.

'Til the Cows Come Home

Often misunderstood, the issue is one of cows and when they come home.

As dairy farmers will tell you there is nothing more regular than a milk cow in need of milking. (FYI: It happens twice a day!)

Most assume the phrase involves an evening ritual when cows return home for the day. But to be clear, this is not the time frame to which the expression refers. Given a four a.m. wake-up call, those late afternoon milkings are nothing compared to the pre-dawn mooing of a milk cow in need.

So next time someone tells you *"We're here 'til the cows come home~"* don't make plans for happy hour. Set your clock; get some rest.

Here 'til the cows come home refers, not to the end of the day, but to the pre-dawn return of a milk cow in udder despair.

Too Many Irons in the Fire

Think pre-electricity, when heavy irons placed among glowing embers made for fiery hot tools.

As temporary heat was given off by any given iron, several were used in rotation, hot replacing cold throughout the ironing process.

As you might imagine, it was no small feat to keep up with which iron was which (for you couldn't tell by color, which ones were still hot). And what's more, heating any one iron for too long was a sure-fire guarantee to scorch a garment.

Too many irons in the fire was more confusing than you might think, often consuming more energy in deliberation than in doing the task itself. By the same token, we use the phrase today to suggest a person who's just way too busy to keep up with what's what.

(in) Two Shakes of a Lamb's Tail

Granted, while a lamb *is* known to shake its tail twice as fast as most any other animal, this particular expression, *in two shakes of a lamb's tail*, seems to be an extension of a more popular British phrase, *in two shakes*.

Both refer to something done in an instantaneous amount of time. Yet, one was coined in the mid 1800s and refers to a small sheep, while the other dates back much further, and has to do with the quick shaking of a dice box, just before those dice are rolled.

"I'm Baaaack..."
(Can you see my tail?)

Up for Grabs

This one comes to us compliments of the Great Depression, when diners and cafeterias found it necessary to save every scrap of food.

At a time when any and all excess was salvaged, restaurant owners soon started setting aside their leftovers for beggars and the homeless. It became customary for these leftover scraps to be set at the end of the lunch counter, bagged and ready to go for anyone who might be in need.

From this, the expression *up for grabs* became the catch phrase for those morsels of food, set *up* on the counter for the needy to *grab*.

The Willies

First cousins with the heebie jeebies, *the willies* likewise convey a state of anxiety or restless concern (i.e., the creeps).

The origins are vague though references point to certain English literary sources that credit the willow (as in Weeping Willow) ...the prosaic symbol for mourning.

Others credit the 19th century ballet, Giselle, in which the heroine is possessed by Wilis (i.e., spirits of beautiful girls who died before their wedding day) found dancing out their anger at the fate that befell them.

References to *the willies* today are less about grief, more akin to nervousness or un-explainable agitation.

Still and so, when someone gives you *the willies*, there is no mistaking the foreboding feeling, some would liken unto a sixth sense, foreshadowing something bad to come.

Y'all

Now in case you aren't from the South, there's one last word you need to know to get you through most any social occasion -- that word is *Y'all*.

Short for *you all*, technically *y'all* is a contraction (which means we slapped two words together to make it happen.)

More important is the spirit of the word.

Y'all is our friendly way of saying "You're like kin!" (And face it, *y'all* is just so much friendlier than *you*, *you all*, or [heaven forbid] *yous guys*.)

But just to make sure you know all there is to know about this figure of speech (that you won't find in your grammar books) well, here's what's what.

Y'all is what you say when referring to a big ol' group of non specific people, (i.e., "Now *y'all* hurry back!") But it's also an endearing term for when speaking to just an inner, close few (i.e., "*Y'all* bring your mother 'n 'em next time.")

But most of all, *y'all* is the Southerner's polite way of including you in our group. (When in doubt, remember the Beverly Hillbillies, "*Y'all* come back now, ya hear!")

Oh. And the plural of *y'all* (in case you're ever asked) is *"All y'all!"*

126

INDEX

INDEX

About the Author

Karlen Evins is a writer, producer and talk show host with a journalism career spanning twenty years. Her interviews range from the political to the spiritual to the mystical and unknown.

A lifelong Tennessean, Karlen lives in Nashville with her two pups, Ike and Minsky. She enjoys writing, yoga and renovating houses.

Also Available in the "I Didn't Know That" Series:

I Didn't Know That comes from the Bible:
from Sour Grapes to Feet of Clay
Biblical Origins Behind Everyday
Words and Expressions

I Didn't Know That's
Southern to the Core
A Heapin' Helpin' of Country Cookin'
(with Southern Sayin's on the Side)

K Rose
publishing

For more information on books, columns and radio features
visit www.karlenevins.com